REMARKABLE PEOPLE

Bono

by Sheelagh Matthews

Published by Weigl Publishers Inc.
350 5th Avenue, Suite 3304, PMB 6G
New York, NY 10118-0069

Website: www.weigl.com
Copyright ©2008 WEIGL PUBLISHERS INC.

All of the Internet URLs given in the book were valid at the time of publication.
However, due to the dynamic nature of the Internet, some addresses may have
changed, or sites may have ceased to exist since publication. While the author and
publisher regret any inconvenience this may cause readers, no responsibility for any
such changes can be accepted by either the author or the publisher.

Library of Congress Cataloging-in-Publication Data

Matthews, Sheelagh.
 Bono / Sheelagh Matthews.
    p. cm. -- (Remarkable people)
 Includes index.
 ISBN 978-1-59036-637-0 (hard cover : alk. paper) -- 978-1-59036-638-7 (soft cover
: alk. paper)
 1. Bono, 1960---Juvenile literature. 2. Rock musicians--Biography--Juvenile
literature. I. Title.
 ML3930.B592M37 2008
 782.42166092--dc22
 [B]
                                       2006039437

Printed in the United States of America
1 2 3 4 5 6 7 8 9 0 11 10 09 08 07

Editor: Leia Tait
Design: Terry Paulhus

Cover: Many people admire Bono for his musical abilities and his efforts to
help others.

Every reasonable effort has been made to trace ownership and to obtain
permission to reprint copyright material. The publishers would be pleased to
have any errors or omissions brought to their attention so that they may be
corrected in subsequent printings.

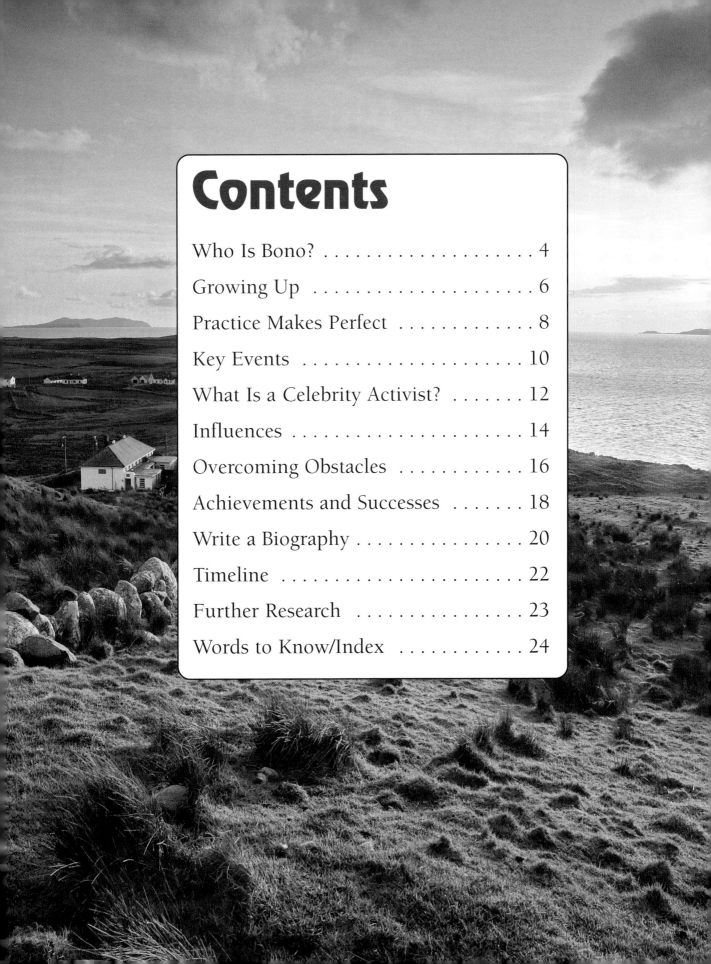

Contents

Who Is Bono?

Bono is the lead singer for the band U2. He writes many of the band's songs. Bono's talents have helped U2 become one of

> "Music can change the world because it can change people."

the world's best-known rock bands. Bono also is known for his efforts to improve the lives of others. He uses his status as a **celebrity** to draw attention to world problems, such as poverty and disease. Bono focuses most of his efforts on helping the people of Africa. He believes it is possible to end poverty in that region of the world. He wants to stop the spread of **AIDS**. Bono has helped raise millions of dollars to accomplish these goals. He has inspired others to join him in this work.

Growing Up

Bono's real name is Paul David Hewson. He was born in Dublin, Ireland on May 10, 1960. Bono has a brother, Norman, who is eight years older than him. When he was growing up, Bono's family was different from most Irish families he knew. His parents, Bobby and Iris, did not share the same religion. Bobby was **Roman Catholic**. Iris was **Protestant**. This was unusual in Ireland at that time. Irish Roman Catholics and Irish Protestants often did not get along. Bono did not understand this conflict. Growing up with parents who practiced different religions taught Bono how two different points of view can exist together in peace.

■ Dublin is built on the River Liffey. The river flows through the city on its way to the Irish Sea.

Get to Know Ireland

SYMBOL
Harp

FLAG

FLOWER
Shamrock

0   190 Miles
0   300 Kilometers

Ireland is part of an island in northwestern Europe. It is bordered by Northern Ireland, which is part of the United Kingdom.

Ireland's most important national holiday is Saint Patrick's Day, which takes place on March 17. It honors Saint Patrick, a key figure in Irish history.

Ireland is sometimes called the "Emerald Isle" for its lush, green vegetation.

Dublin is the capital city of Ireland.

The Connemara pony is the only type of horse that is native to Ireland.

Think about it!

Ireland is Bono's homeland. People, places, and events in Ireland often inspire Bono as a songwriter. Think about the place where you live. What people, places or events are important to you? What do you want others to know about your country? Try writing a poem, a song, or a short story about your homeland.

Practice Makes Perfect

In Dublin, Bono attended Glasnevin National Primary School, and later, Saint Patrick's Secondary School for Boys. He was a curious student. His favorite subjects were history, art, and drama. Bono belonged to many clubs and associations. He enjoyed meeting new people and having fun with others.

In 1972, Bono began attending Mount Temple Comprehensive School. This was the first school in Dublin to allow children from different religious groups to attend the same school. While there, Bono became interested in music. One day in 1976, he saw a note on the school bulletin board. It was written by Larry Mullen, Jr., another student at the school. Larry was looking for musicians to form a rock band. Bono was excited about this. He wanted to join the band.

■ Bono and Larry Mullen, Jr., are still band mates today. Larry was only 14 when he decided to start a band at Mount Temple School.

Along with Bono, three other students wanted to join Larry's band. Their names were Adam Clayton, Dave Evans, and Dick Evans. Dave and Dick were brothers. The boys formed a band called "Feedback." Bono became the lead singer. Larry played drums. Adam played bass guitar, and Dave and Dick played rhythm guitar.

The band began practicing many nights at school and in the garden shed at the Evans' home. First, they played well-known songs by other bands. Over time, they began to write their own music. Soon, they were playing small shows. In 1978, the band won a talent show in the city of Limerick, Ireland. One of the judges at the show was Jackie Hayden. He worked in the music business in Ireland. Jackie helped the band record their first **demo**. Shortly after, Dick Evans left to join a different band.

■ Early in his career, Bono taught himself to play the guitar.

Key Events

After Dick left the band, Bono, Larry, Adam, and Dave renamed their group U2. With hard work, they began to make themselves known in the music business. In September 1979, their first song was played on Irish radio stations. It was called *U2-3*. The following year, U2 signed its first international record deal with Island Records. Soon, Bono and his band mates were recording their first record album, called *Boy*. The record was released in October 1980. Since then, U2 has made many more albums and sold more than 150 million copies of them. They are now one of the most successful bands in the world.

During the 1970s and 1980s, the human rights group **Amnesty** International organized a series of **benefit concerts** in Great Britain. The concerts were called the Secret Policeman's Balls. Bono attended one of the early concerts. He saw that music can do more than entertain people. He realized that musicians can inspire others to change the world. Bono began to think about how he could use his music to help others.

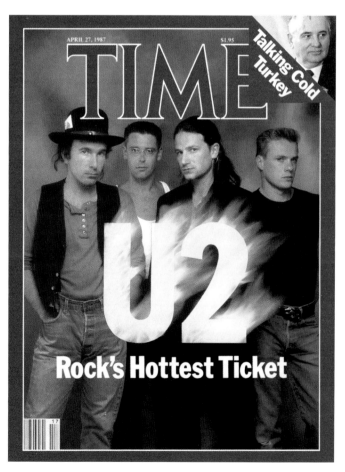

■ U2 appeared on the cover of *Time* magazine on April 27, 1987. That same week, *The Joshua Tree* became the band's first record to reach number one in U.S. sales.

Thoughts from Bono

Bono has said many things about his music and his desire to help others. Here are some examples.

Bono grows up in Dublin.

"I knew that we were different on our street because my mother was Protestant. And that she'd married a Catholic [...] I knew that was special."

Bono becomes interested in helping others.

"I saw The Secret Policeman's Ball and it became a part of me. It sowed a seed..."

Bono urges Americans to help stop the spread of AIDS in Africa.

"This is a chance for the United States to redescribe itself to the rest of the world, show its greatness, and respond to what is the greatest health emergency in 600 years."

Bono is inspired by others.

"My heroes are the ones who survived doing it wrong, who made mistakes, but recovered from them."

Bono has two important goals.

"As a rock star, I have two **instincts**—I want to have fun, and I want to change the world. I have a chance to do both."

Bono has a natural talent for writing songs.

"My actual gift is I wake up in the morning with melodies in my head and then I sing them."

What Is a Celebrity Activist?

An activist works for a cause to solve a problem or to make the world a better place. Social activists work to help people in need, such as those who are poor or sick. Other activists may work to protect the environment or help animals. Some activists **volunteer** for a cause they care about. Others make it a career.

Many people who are celebrities also are activists. They use their fame and influence to draw attention to important causes. During U2 concerts, Bono reminds fans about poverty and disease in Africa. Like many celebrity activists, he promotes **charity** campaigns and makes public speeches. Bono speaks to reporters to help educate people about issues that are important to him. Celebrity activists often meet with other influential people to share ideas and make plans for action.

■ Bono often works with other celebrity activists, such as Beyonce Knowles. In 2003, they visited South Africa to draw attention to AIDS issues in the region.

Celebrity Activists 101

Bob Geldof (1954–)

Cause: Africa

Achievements: Bob Geldof is a musician from Ireland. He has helped organize many important music projects for charity. In 1984, he created Band Aid. This project brought together well-known British and Irish musicians to record the song, *Do They Know It's Christmas?* Money from sales of the song was used to help feed starving people in Africa. The following year, Geldof organized a series of benefit concerts called Live Aid. The concerts raised more than $245 million in aid for Africa. In 2005, Geldof organized Live 8, another series of benefit concerts to help Africa.

Angelina Jolie (1975–)

Cause: Refugees

Achievements: Angelina Jolie is one of the world's best-known actors. She is also a social activist. In 2001, Jolie became a Goodwill **Ambassador** for the Office of the **United Nations** High Commissioner for Refugees (UNHCR). In this role, Jolie raises money to aid refugees who are fleeing dangers and difficulties in their homelands. She also travels around the world to visit refugees in Cambodia, Tanzania, Pakistan, Thailand, Ecuador, and many other places. Through these visits, Jolie hopes to make others aware of the hardships people face when they are forced to leave their homes.

Sarah McLachlan (1968–)

Cause: Women's issues, poverty

Achievements: Sarah McLachlan is an award-winning Canadian singer and songwriter. In 1996, she organized Lilith Fair. This concert tour of women music artists raised money for women's charities in each location it visited. The tour raised more than $7 million for other charity groups across North America. These included Amnesty International, the National Organization for Women (NOW) and the Breast Cancer Fund. In 2004, McLachlan used the $150,00 budget for a music video to improve the lives of people around the world.

Leonardo DiCaprio (1974–)

Cause: The environment

Achievements: Leonardo DiCaprio is an award-winning actor and environmental activist. He formed his own activist group in 1998. The Leonardo DiCaprio Foundation helps educate people about issues such as **global warming**. It gives money to help scientists find new energy sources that will not harm the environment. The foundation also helps protect animals. DiCaprio speaks about these issues at important events. He helps produce films to educate viewers about the environment. In 2001, his foundation received the Martin Litton Environmental Warrior Award from an organization called Environment Now.

The Campaign

A campaign is a series of actions that are planned and carried out to bring about a particular result. Activists use campaigns to draw attention to the issues they are concerned about. Sometimes, campaigns are aimed at improving people's knowledge of an issue. These are called public awareness campaigns. Other campaigns might urge people to take specific actions. Effective communication is necessary in order for a campaign to be successful.

Influences

Bono enjoys music and is often inspired by other musicians. Growing up, he admired rock bands such as the Beatles, the Rolling Stones, and the Beach Boys. Later, he enjoyed **punk rock**. Bono thought this kind of music allowed people to express themselves in a way they had not done before.

When U2 formed, the band struggled to create its own style of rock and roll music. At the time, Bono was listening to the music of another rock and roll artist, Bruce Springsteen. Bono admired Springsteen's ability to write meaningful songs. Like Springsteen, Bono and the other members of U2 wanted to write songs that had an important message. Bono began to write songs about the religious and social **injustices** he saw around him. He used his songs to express his feelings about these issues. Bono's songs helped U2 become well known.

■ Bruce Springsteen is a U.S. rock and roll artist. He is well known for his songs about the challenges of daily life.

In 1984, Bono sang in Bob Geldof's Band Aid project. This was the beginning of his activism work for Africa. The next year, Bono joined Geldof again to sing at Live Aid. The two became close friends. Since then, they have worked to improve life for people in Africa. Together, Bono and Geldof have drawn attention to problems, such as poverty, starvation, and AIDS, in that region of the world. In 2005, they worked together once again to help organize Live 8.

AIDS IN AFRICA

AIDS is a greater problem in Africa than any other place in the world. More than 6,000 people in Africa die of this disease every day. Millions of children in that region have lost their parents to AIDS. This has worsened other problems in the region, such as poverty and starvation. More than 4 million people in Africa who are suffering from AIDS do not have access to medicines that can help them. Bono and other activists work to make these medicines available to everyone who needs them. They educate people in Africa about AIDS to help stop the spread of this disease. Many activists work closely with the people of Africa to find the best solutions to the region's problems.

■ Many people in Africa are excited about efforts to stop the spread of AIDS. In Kenya, women use their craft skills to help raise awareness about this disease.

Overcoming Obstacles

Bono is now a successful musician and activist, but he has faced many obstacles in his life. When he was 14, Bono's mother, Iris, died suddenly. This was a difficult time for Bono. He was sad that his mother was gone. He was angry that he would not be able to know her better as he grew older. Bono struggled with these feelings for many years. To help make sense of his feelings, Bono wrote songs. Many U2 songs focus on Bono's experience with his mother's death.

■ Bono uses singing and songwriting to help him overcome difficult times in his life, such as his mother's death.

After Bono's mother died, he did not get along with his father, Bobby. The two disagreed about many things, especially Bono's musical goals. Unlike Bono, Bobby loved opera. He enjoyed singing **tenor**. However, Bobby never had the opportunity to become a professional singer or learn to play the piano. This made him very disappointed. When Bono became interested in music, Bobby did not encourage him. Bobby did not believe that Bono would be successful. He thought Bono would only be disappointed, like he was. Bono was hurt by his father's comments. He decided to prove Bobby wrong. Bono set big goals for himself and for U2. Overcoming his father's negative thinking helped Bono become the success that he is today.

■ Today, Bono receives support and encouragement from his wife, Alison. They enjoy spending time with their children, Jordan, Memphis Eve, Elijah, and John.

Achievements and Successes

Bono has had many successes. With U2, he has won many music awards, including more than 20 Grammy Awards. These awards are given out by professionals in the U.S. music industry to recognize outstanding achievement in music. In 2005, Bono and his U2 band mates became members of the Rock and Roll Hall of Fame.

Through his music and activism, Bono has met some of the world's most influential people. These include former U.S. Presidents Bill Clinton and George Bush, U.S. President George W. Bush, and British Prime Minister Tony Blair. In 1999, Bono met the leader of the Roman Catholic Church at the time, Pope John Paul II. At their meeting, the Pope traded his **rosary** for a pair of Bono's sunglasses.

■ In February 2006, Bono met with U.S. President George W. Bush and other important leaders to request their help in Africa.

Bono has won many awards for his work as an activist. He was named one of *Time* magazine's Persons of the Year in 2005. He was nominated for the Nobel Peace Prize in 2003, 2005, and 2006. In 2006, Queen Elizabeth II of Great Britain awarded Bono an honorary knighthood. This is a title of merit given to non-British individuals who have contributed to Great Britain with their achievements. Each of these awards recognize Bono's many efforts on behalf of Africa through Live 8, Amnesty International, and Bono's own foundation, Debt, AIDS, Trade, Africa (DATA).

DEBT, AIDS, TRADE, AFRICA (DATA)

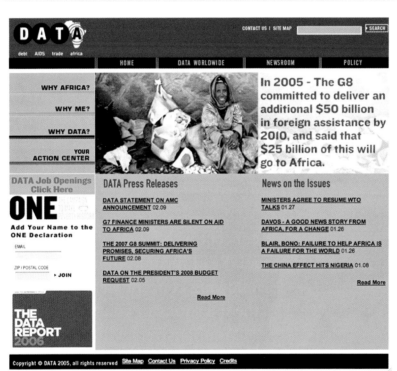

Debt, AIDS, Trade, Africa (DATA) is an organization started by Bono and other activists in 2002. It educates people about the hardships currently affecting Africa. Its members urge governments in other countries to give money to help solve Africa's problems. They help plan new ways for people in Africa to overcome the challenges that have caused these problems. DATA teaches individuals and governments around the world about how they can help people in Africa. To learn more about DATA, visit their website at **www.data.org**.

Write a Biography

A person's life story can be the subject of a book. This kind of book is called a biography. Biographies describe the lives of remarkable people, such as those who have achieved great success or have done important things to help others. These people may be alive today or they may have lived many years ago. Reading a biography can help you learn more about a remarkable person.

At school, you might be asked to write a biography. First, decide who you want to write about. You can choose a celebrity activist, such as Bono, or any other person you find interesting. Then, find out if your library has any books about this person. Learn as much as you can about him or her. Write down the key events in this person's life. What was this person's childhood like? What has he or she accomplished? What are his or her goals? What makes this person special or unusual?

A concept web is a useful research tool. Read the questions in the following concept web. Answer the questions in your notebook. Your answers will help you write your biography review.

• Where does this individual currently reside?
• Does he or she have a family?

• What did you learn from the books you read in your research?
• Would you suggest these books to others?
• Was anything missing from these books?

• Where and when was this person born?
• Describe his or her parents, siblings, and friends.
• Did this person grow up in unusual circumstances?

Your Opinion

Adulthood

Childhood

WRITING A BIOGRAPHY

Main Accomplishments

Help and Obstacles

Work and Preparation

• What is this person's life's work?
• Has he or she received awards or recognition for accomplishments?
• How have this person's accomplishments served others?

• What was this person's education?
• What was his or her work experience?
• How does this person work; what is or was the process he or she uses or used?

• Did this individual have a positive attitude?
• Did he or she receive help from others?
• Did this person have a **mentor**?
• Did this person face any hardships?
• If so, how were the hardships overcome?

Timeline

YEAR	BONO	WORLD EVENTS
1960	Paul David Hewson is born on May 10 in Dublin, Ireland.	John F. Kennedy is elected president of the United States on November 8.
1976	Bono and four friends form the band that would later become U2.	10,000 Protestant and Catholic women march for peace in Northern Ireland on August 14.
1984	On November 25, Bono sings with Band Aid to raise money for Africa.	Ethiopia, a country in Africa, faces an extreme shortage of food. Nearly one million people die from starvation.
1999	Bono meets with Pope John Paul II on September 23 to discuss the struggles of the world's poorest regions, including Africa.	The world's population reaches 6 billion.
2002	Bono helps creates Debt, AIDS, Trade, Africa (DATA) to help end poverty and AIDS in Africa.	Former U.S. President Jimmy Carter wins the Nobel Peace Prize for his efforts to end global conflicts and promote human rights.
2005	Bono helps Bob Geldof organize Live 8. *Time* magazine names Bono one of three Persons of the Year.	Hurricane Katrina strikes the U.S. Gulf Coast on August 29.
2007	Queen Elizabeth II of Great Britain chooses Bono to receive an honorary knighthood.	On January 29, the U.S. government gives $4.5 billion to help fight AIDS in Africa and other struggling countries.

Further Research

How can I find out more about Bono?

Most libraries have computers that connect to a database for searching for information. If you input a key word, you will be provided with a list of books in the library that contain information on that topic. Non-fiction books are arranged numerically, using their call number. Fiction books are organized alphabetically by the author's last name.

Websites

To learn more about Bono and U2, visit
www.u2.com

To learn more about youth activism, visit
www.freechild.org

Words to Know

AIDS: Acquired Immune Deficiency Syndrome; a serious disease that destroys the body's ability to fight illnesses

ambassador: an official representative

amnesty: forgiving or overlooking past offenses

benefit concerts: performances or shows given to raise money for a charitable cause

celebrity: a very well-known person

charity: giving money or help to those in need

demo: a trial recording of a song or album that is used to attract interest from record companies, musicians, and other artists

global warming: warming of Earth's temperature due to air pollution and the destruction of the ozone layer

injustices: acts of unfairness

instincts: natural ways of behaving

mentor: a wise and trusted teacher

Protestant: a member of any Christian church other than the Roman Catholic Church or the Orthodox Church

punk rock: a loud form of rock music expressing anger and social separation

refugees: people flee for safety, especially to a foreign country

Roman Catholic: a member of the Christian church that recognizes the pope as its leader

rosary: a string of beads used in reciting prayers

tenor: the second-lowest part in a four-part musical harmony; between bass and alto

United Nations (UN): a peace organization made up of many of the world's countries

volunteer: work for no pay

Index